a Week at the Lake

a Week at the Lake

GRACE BUTTERFIELD DOW

Wood Engravings by Siri Beckman

Down East Books

Wood engravings © 1998 by Siri Beckman

Text © 1998, 2001, by Nan Mulford

Design for this edition by Darel Gabriel Bridges

ISBN 0-89272-525-7

Library of Congress Catalog Card Number: 00-111616

2   4   5   3   1

Down East Books, P.O. Box 679, Camden ME 04843

Book orders: (800) 766-1670

Printed in China

PREFACE

What follows is a faithful transcription of my mother Grace's diary containing the account of a week that she and my father spent at Witipitlock Lake, in the northeastern part of Maine, in the fall of 1932. I heard much about the lake as I was growing up, and she always described it as a magical place. It is still a remote spot. For purposes of clarity, some punctuation, shifts in tense, and a few misspellings have been corrected (except for "sandwitches," which I remember so dearly from her pen).

My mother and father lived in Augusta, Maine, in this first year of their marriage, but since the first diary entry mentions the sunrise over the harbor, they must have started this trip from Rockport, where their families lived and where they had been high school sweethearts. "Bump" was my father's high school nickname, taken, as I recall, from a Booth Tarkington novel. At the time of their first anniversary and this memorable trip to Witipitlock, my mother was twenty-six years old.

My mother's father, whom she remembers fondly in the diary, was a forester who spent a great deal of time in the Maine woods. He died of typhoid fever when she was eight years old, leaving my grandmother, Muz, with five children, aged eight to fifteen.

As far as I know, my mother never returned to Witipitlock Lake. I was born two years later, and about three years after that she fell ill with tuberculosis. This began a lifetime of ill health, culminating in a long bout with cancer, from which she died in 1960, at the age of fifty-four. Looking back, I see that her concluding words in the Witipitlock diary were poignantly prophetic: "... I realize that there will be changes come to us—trials and hardships. There may never be just this kind of carefree, unaware happiness we have known or this special close togetherness."

She was a rare person, loved by all, and possessing a wonderful sense of irony and humor, a true artistic gift of expression, and a love of nature and its creatures, including humans. I miss her still.

Nan Dow Mulford
November 2000

First
Wedding Anniversary
of
Grace Butterfield
and
Francis P. Dow

⤻

at Witipitlock, Maine.
October 21, 1932

FRIDAY, OCTOBER 21

⌐⌐

    We left home this morning just as the sun came up over the harbor. Such a perfect autumn day. That crisp little chilly tang in the air and gusts of bright leaves blowing across the road before the car. The beautiful drive up the shoreline. We were so happy and excited and contented, with no cares or obligations left behind or worries of the future. The joy of being young and full of health and together. I was so thrilled with my new hunting boots and the feel of my lovely new whipcord breeches. The back of the car held a big box of provisions for one week's stay in the woods, and when we stopped and ate our lunch of hot coffee, big sandwitches, and doughnuts, it tasted like food for gods.

    We got to Witipitlock in the late afternoon, and I met these nice friends of Bump's: Glen and Pearl. They seem to think a great deal of him and were very surprised and pleased to meet his bride. They invited us to use their camp, which is three miles by motorboat and about fifteen by the shore path from the inlet and the nearest camp on the lake. So we consider ourselves very lucky indeed. We all drove to the lake together. They are coming too, to stay the weekend. Pearl had a big fresh-baked pot of beans and hot biscuits.

Just at dusk we all crowded in the big boat for camp. A high wind had sprung up when the sun went down, and black clouds scudded across the sky. The great, brooding, shadowy forest crowded the lake's edge and stretched on either side as far as my eyes could see. Here was no peaceful, calm little lake with loons calling at evening but an almost forbidding scene that made me realize we were far from civilization and this a real wilderness. And right then I knew I loved it all beyond anything and had

 a strange feeling of familiarity with it. Perhaps an inheritance from Papa, because of his great love for the woods and the many years he spent in them. The memories all came back to me, clear and vivid, of those summers when Muz took Doris and me, just little girls, away into the woods to be with Papa.

At last we reached the camp. A snug, little low-roofed place on the shore of the lake looking so cozy and welcoming against the dark background of forest. The door opens on its hinges with a squeak, and an earthy tarred-paper smell rushes out into the chill night. There's the little kitchen with a low window looking out on the lake, and a long table with benches under it. The sink, the cupboard, and a big old rusty range that bakes like the most expensive

electric one. The men soon had a hot fire there and the beans on heating. There's a little window over the sink that looks out at the small clearing and the wood pile and the sunny trail that leads away to the dim woods. The living room is sweet, with windows on the lake side, and couches, and the walls hung with deer horns and gun racks. There's a bulging old wood-fired heater that they cram full of great chunks, and it roars away, giving off big blasts of heat. There are two bunk rooms with double tiers of bunks piled high with homemade quilts and wool blankets. They smell like wood-smoke and sunlight and spruce.

This has been a lovely day—every minute. I suppose I cannot realize how sweet, but someday I may look back and wonder at that gay, happy time. I go to bed in the bunk beside Bump with my long-legged union suit on and welcome the pile of warm quilts. I drop off to dreamless

sleep hearing the wind scrape the tree branches over the low roof. I have a glimpse of stars in a pool of black sky through the little window over the bunk.

SATURDAY, OCTOBER 22

❧

We got up at 4:30 this morning. It is the best time to get a deer—before sun-up. Bump went off with the two men and I stayed around the camp—exploring and visiting with Pearl, who was busy all the morning making a wonderful venison stew. I sat on the little porch and dreamed out at the lake. The waves sparkling like stars. Such a bright day. After dinner I went out with Bump into the Real Woods, and I wish I could give expression to my real impressions.

We are pygmies in a world of giants—benevolent giants with the peace of great wisdom. Tangled underbrush and

old blazed logging trails. Beech, Ash, Birch, Spruce—the
wind sighing among their branches with a low, continuous
murmur. No other sound but a blue jay's harsh call, the
sudden chatter of squirrels, or the weird cry of a moose-
bird. Sunny beech ridges and trails that lead away between

aisles of the great giants.
Here the sun never quite
penetrates the still, brown
avenues where footsteps are
muffled in leaves going back
to their fathers.

We carved our initials in
two birches and followed an
old trail for miles. We rested
on fallen logs, warm in the
sun, and Bump smoked
away on his old pipe, his

9

eyes ever on the alert for a deer and his rifle ready across his knees. But I just sat and basked and dreamed and let that delicious Fall smell of dying leaves sink into my every pore. We do not talk ever—there is something about it here that makes talking seem unnecessary.

When the shadows began to lengthen, we took our way back to camp and found the folks all ready to start for home. I stood on the porch and watched their boat out of sight on the lake and had a queer little sinking feeling when I realized we were alone here so very far from people. But the cozy cheer of the camp soon dispelled all that, and I got us a supper of venison fit for a king.

Glen gave us a whole hind-quarter of a young lamb. We are going to bed early tonight because tomorrow we will be up long before daylight.

Sunday, October 23

～

Up and out in the woods before the sun. A heavy frost covered the ground. It was bitterly cold and dead still except for the tiny chipmunks busily scurrying for fallen beechnuts and our boots crunching the frosty, stiff leaves underfoot.

I walk a bit behind Bump and feel tense and alive for the slightest motion or sound that means "A Deer!" I try to walk as quietly as he but fail miserably, and the twig that snaps beneath my boot sounds like a cannon, and he turns and glares at me, and I feel guilty because I know I am only here on suffrage—it is really a man's world, this one of hunting. But I have it in my blood as strong as any man and so can't resist being with him. For all his weight, he walks so quietly and seems to know where to step without looking. His eyes shine and his face blazes with color and his hands look frozen cold on his rifle but he wears no gloves or mittens and never complains of the cold. He is so alive up here—I am getting acquainted with a new personality in him.

At noon we came upon a clearing and an old logging camp rotting away and eaten by hedgehogs. We sat in the old doorway and dreamed in the noonday stillness. Ate our lunch, and I chewed spruce gum. We wondered about the hordes of woodsmen who long ago made camp there. There, almost buried in tall grass, dry and sere, was the old horse stable, there the cook's house, and here the big shack for the men. The noise and bustle and life, and now—long,

long after—this still, small space in the great woods. The place where the shy, elusive deer bed down in the tall grass and wily old hedgehogs explore. Off in the pines the thrushes call. Slowly but inevitably, the forest creeping back to claim its own. This land wild and not for man.

Back to camp at dusk, and Bump made flapjacks for our supper. It is so still and frosty out tonight. Twigs snap, and the tall trees around the camp stand dreaming in the bleak moonlight.

Monday, October 24

We were in the little old rowboat out on the lake this morning just before the sun came up. Going to hunt on the opposite shore. A half inch of frost covered the boat and the ground and thin ice had formed around the edges of the lake overnight. We rowed over to the other side through swirling early-morning mists rising phantom-like from the surface of the lake. Wild ducks clucked and paddled away over near the shore. We landed in tall, frosty marsh grass and made our way slowly up along a beech ridge.

I love it in the early morning. It is so still—those who have never experienced this stillness could never imagine what it is like. As if this woods and this place were not for us—it belongs to all the wild creatures, mysterious and alien. The dying leaves waft slowly down on us in a perfect rain—the little hushing noise as they land the only sound. All around that faint whispering sound. Not a breath of wind. "Before the sun comes up there is grey mist along the wooded slopes, softening the sere leaves underfoot. Gaunt tree trunk and branch and brushwood, austere for the bitter coldness soon to come. And always, on every hand and in each sort of air, the certainty that autumn wanes and winter is drawing close."

Today we ate our lunch lying among the crackling beech leaves in the warm sun and threw bits of bread to the squirrels, who were bold and tame and chattered away to us profanely at our intrusion.

Surely my mind is under a spell of strange enchantment, because as I lie here I think of nothing at all. Not the past or the future but a lazy, dreamy contentment with this moment. Only elemental things have any significance— food and shelter and sleep.

When we got back to the lake shore and our boat, we found a good-sized gale had sprung up, but we decided to risk crossing. Once out, we regretted it. The treacherous lake waves pounded the little boat broadside, and we had only the one oar and no oarlocks. We headed for the nearest shore with real fear gripping our hearts. Each battering wave would seem to be the last before we surely upset. But even in our panic we had to laugh weakly at poor

Bump's clumsy efforts with the unwieldy oar he was trying to use as a paddle. Each time he swung it I got a thump in the head, and between that and my terror of those whitecapped furies I was reduced to helpless laughing— a sure sign I'm good and frightened. At last we made the shore, and I followed it gratefully all the long way to camp with Bump poling the boat along beside me.

A storm is brewing, and the sight of the warm, friendly little camp made my heart leap for joy. A good hot supper restored our spirits. And so to bed, to the sound of the waves breaking on the shore and all the forest creaking in the gale.

TUESDAY, OCTOBER 25

⌘

This morning we slept late and got up to find last night's gale still blowing and the lake a white-capped fury. It's not cold at all, and the air is so fresh and sweet and sprucy smelling. Bump slept away on the couch, and I made us a delicious partridge stew for dinner.

After dinner we went out and spent the whole afternoon following an old trail through a swamp. Spongy moss underfoot and old foot bridges of logs half buried under the moss. Cedar, spruce, and fir, thick matted underbrush. Dim and mysterious—the sun's pale rays seeping down through branches in faint greenish-yellow blurs.

On the way home Bump shot three partridges. One fell right at my feet, and I saw all its wild, proud beauty quiver out like a light. The lids came up over the bright little eyes, and each separate beautiful feather that had seemed to have a life of its own faded, until the bird was just a sodden warm bundle on the ground. I guess I'm not a good hunter, but it is the law of the wild, and I wouldn't dare say these things to Bump. He has a sympathy for the little

wild things too, but he is a hunter first. And I confess I
do like to eat them. Such nice fat partridge breasts fried in
butter for our supper.

Wednesday, October 26

✦

It has been pouring rain all day, but a warm rain. We
have lounged around camp most of the day, but did go out
in the woods for awhile this afternoon. The air so fresh
and clean, and such a delicious smell. I gathered bunches
of pungent spruce boughs to make pillows and had little
piles all along the trail to pick up on our way back. I hunt-
ed for spruce gum. Bump still eager to get a shot at a deer,
but I'm quite relaxed and enjoying the woods and camp
life. When we got home we sat on the porch and cut the
tender buds off the spruce boughs and got sopping wet,
but felt so fresh and warm.

Thursday, October 27

~⟡~

It rained a flood all night, pounding on the roof. So snug and warm and cozy under the old quilts. The roof leaked a little, and we found our bunk getting wet, so we moved in to the other bunk room. In the morning we found the roof leaking over the stove, so it was a job to start the fire.

I hung the bedding up on the rope string in the living room and packed all our things, and soon we heard the *putt-putt* of the motor boat coming. Pearl, Glen, and others. We had a lot of fun and talk before we left with them. I donned Glen's slicker, and we started off with old Gasse in the boat. The water came up rough and wild, and the rain pelted us, but how I loved it—and what a pang of nostalgia to be leaving those wooded shores. All that great silent timberland calling to some answering chord deep in my heart.

At the foot of the lake I went in to Gasse's camp and dried

my shoes and toasted my feet in his oven. Then into the car and on the road home. At Mattawamkeag we hit quite a heavy downfall of snow. The first of the season, and cold.

Here we are coming back to such a different world than we have been knowing up there—so reluctant to take up all the inane things of everyday living. If I had been born a man, I would live all my life long in my beloved woods, far from towns and people. "Far by lonely lakes, silent dusky gorges, mazey thickets, wild sweet woods of birch and hemlock, reedy morasses and solitary brakes."

This time will never quite repeat itself, although we may often steal away together to be alone in this place we love, for I realize that there will be changes come to us—trials and hardships. There may never be just this kind of care-free, unaware happiness we have known or this special close togetherness. And now there are only memories left, but memories that will live with me always.

About Witipitlock Lake

The lake is located about fifteen miles from the Aroostook County town of Wytopitlock (now the official spelling). Its name comes from the Wabanaki, meaning "at the place where there are alders."

A Note about Wood Engraving

Wood engraving is a relief printmaking method with a long history in both art and printing. The concept of engraving (incising a line in a hard material such as stone, metal, or wood) is as old as our Paleolithic ancestors.

Wood engraving is often confused with woodcut, but there are several significant differences. Engraving is done on the end grain of very hard woods such as boxwood or maple. Woodcuts use the plank side of softer woods. Engraving on the end grain allows a fluidity absent in many woodcuts, where the grain of the wood can sometimes pose a problem. The great density of boxwood and maple also permits the cutting of fine detail.

Engraving on wood is done with tools called gravers, which are similar to metal engraving tools. The basic tool is the burin, but at least six other engraving tools come into use during the process.

Each wood engraving takes many hours to complete. For example, a six-by-eight-inch block represents forty to fifty hours of work. Once a block is near completion, I proof it with ink, then fine tune it until the image is as desired. Only then does printing the edition begin. After the edition is printed, it is curated, numbered, and signed.

Siri Beckman, 2001

COLOPHON

The text of the diary is set in ITC Tiepolo, the date
headers are set in Adobe Poetica, incidental text is Adobe
Garamond, and the title is set in Monotype Aldine.

The wood engravings were cut in boxwood,
maple, and Resingrave.

A Week at the Lake was first published in 1998
in a limited, numbered edition of fifty, designed,
hand printed, and bound by Siri Beckman.